Reflections on God's Word

Hearing God's Voice

This journal belongs to:

_____

This journal was started on:

_____

This journal was filled on:

_____

Then the Lord answered me and said,
"Write the vision
And engrave it plainly on [clay] tablets
So that the one who reads it will run.
For the vision is yet for the appointed [future] time
It hurries toward the goal [of fulfillment]; it will not fail.
Even though it delays, wait [patiently] for it,
Because it will certainly come; it will not delay.

-Habakkuk 2:2 (AMP)

Contents

Sections:

Preparation 9

Personal Study 19

Message Notes 61

Section 1
Preparation

Prayer List, Vision, Goals, Blessings

> Trust whatever you do to the Lord, and your plans will be successful.
>
> -Proverbs 16:3 (FBV)

Prayer List

Visions

Goals

Blessings

Section 2
Personal Study

Notes, insights, reflections

> It is to be with him, and he is to read it all the
> days of his life so that he may learn to revere
> the LORD his God and follow carefully all the
> words of this law and these decrees
>
> -Deuteronomy 17:19 (NIV)

Notes

Date: _____

Bible Verse: _____

What is God revealing:

_____

_____

_____

_____

_____

How does this apply to my situation:

_____

_____

_____

_____

_____

Notes

Date: _____

Bible Verse: _____

What is God revealing:

_____

_____

_____

_____

How does this apply to my situation:

_____

_____

_____

_____

Notes

Date: _____

Bible Verse: _____

What is God revealing:

_____

_____

_____

_____

_____

How does this apply to my situation:

_____

_____

_____

_____

_____

Notes

Date: _____

Bible Verse: _____

What is God revealing:

_____

_____

_____

_____

How does this apply to my situation:

_____

_____

_____

_____

_____

Notes

Date: _____

Bible Verse: _____

What is God revealing:

_____

_____

_____

_____

How does this apply to my situation:

_____

_____

_____

_____

Notes

Date: _____

Bible Verse: _____

What is God revealing:

_____

_____

_____

_____

How does this apply to my situation:

_____

_____

_____

_____

Notes

Date: _____

Bible Verse: _____

What is God revealing:

_____

_____

_____

_____

_____

How does this apply to my situation:

_____

_____

_____

_____

_____

Notes

Date: _____

Bible Verse: _____

What is God revealing:

_____

_____

_____

_____

How does this apply to my situation:

_____

_____

_____

_____

Notes

Date: _____

Bible Verse: _____

What is God revealing:

_____

_____

_____

_____

How does this apply to my situation:

_____

_____

_____

_____

_____

Notes

Date: _____

Bible Verse: _____

What is God revealing:

_____

_____

_____

_____

_____

How does this apply to my situation:

_____

_____

_____

_____

_____

Notes

Date: _____

Bible Verse: _____

What is God revealing:

_____

_____

_____

_____

_____

How does this apply to my situation:

_____

_____

_____

_____

_____

Notes

Date: _____

Bible Verse: _____

What is God revealing:

_____
_____
_____
_____
_____

How does this apply to my situation:

_____
_____
_____
_____
_____

Notes

Date: _____

Bible Verse: _____

What is God revealing:

_____

_____

_____

_____

_____

How does this apply to my situation:

_____

_____

_____

_____

_____

Notes

Date: _____

Bible Verse: _____

What is God revealing:

_____

_____

_____

_____

_____

How does this apply to my situation:

_____

_____

_____

_____

_____

Notes

Date: _____

Bible Verse: _____

What is God revealing:

_____

_____

_____

_____

_____

How does this apply to my situation:

_____

_____

_____

_____

_____

Notes

Date: _____

Bible Verse: _____

What is God revealing:

_____

_____

_____

_____

_____

How does this apply to my situation:

_____

_____

_____

_____

_____

Notes

Date: _____

Bible Verse: _____

What is God revealing:

_____

_____

_____

_____

_____

How does this apply to my situation:

_____

_____

_____

_____

_____

Notes

Date: _____

Bible Verse: _____

What is God revealing:

_____

_____

_____

_____

_____

How does this apply to my situation:

_____

_____

_____

_____

_____

Notes

Date: _____

Bible Verse: _____

What is God revealing:

_____

_____

_____

_____

_____

How does this apply to my situation:

_____

_____

_____

_____

_____

Notes

Date: _____

Bible Verse: _____

What is God revealing:

_____

_____

_____

_____

How does this apply to my situation:

_____

_____

_____

_____

Section 3
Message Notes

Highlights, insights, reflections

> But blessed are your eyes because they see, and your ears because they hear.17For truly I tell you, many prophets and righteous people longed to see what you see but did not see it, and to hear what you hear but did not hear it.
>
> -Matthew 13:16-17 (NIV)

Notes

Date: _____ Pastor/Communicator: _____

Message Title: _____

_____

_____

_____

_____

_____

_____

_____

_____

_____

_____

_____

_____

_____

What is God revealing:
_____
_____
_____
_____

How does this apply to my situation:
_____
_____
_____
_____

What actions will I take:
_____
_____
_____
_____

Notes

Date: _____   Pastor/Communicator: _____

Message Title: _____

_____

_____

_____

_____

_____

_____

_____

_____

_____

_____

_____

_____

_____

What is God revealing:

_____
_____
_____
_____

How does this apply to my situation:

_____
_____
_____
_____

What actions will I take:

_____
_____
_____
_____

Notes

Date: _____ Pastor/Communicator: _____

Message Title: _____

_____
_____
_____
_____
_____
_____
_____
_____
_____
_____
_____
_____
_____

What is God revealing:

_____

_____

_____

_____

_____

How does this apply to my situation:

_____

_____

_____

_____

_____

What actions will I take:

_____

_____

_____

_____

_____

Notes

Date: _____   Pastor/Communicator: _____

Message Title: _____

_____
_____
_____
_____
_____
_____
_____
_____
_____
_____
_____
_____
_____
_____
_____

What is God revealing:

_____

_____

_____

_____

How does this apply to my situation:

_____

_____

_____

_____

What actions will I take:

_____

_____

_____

_____

Notes

Date: _____   Pastor/Communicator: _____

Message Title: _____

_____
_____
_____
_____
_____
_____
_____
_____
_____
_____
_____
_____
_____
_____

What is God revealing:

_____
_____
_____
_____

How does this apply to my situation:

_____
_____
_____
_____

What actions will I take:

_____
_____
_____
_____

Notes

Date: _____   Pastor/Communicator: _____

Message Title: _____

_____
_____
_____
_____
_____
_____
_____
_____
_____
_____
_____
_____
_____

What is God revealing:

_____
_____
_____
_____
_____

How does this apply to my situation:

_____
_____
_____
_____
_____

What actions will I take:

_____
_____
_____
_____
_____

Notes

Date: _____   Pastor/Communicator: _____

Message Title: _____

_____
_____
_____
_____
_____
_____
_____
_____
_____
_____
_____
_____
_____
_____
_____
_____

What is God revealing:

_____
_____
_____
_____

How does this apply to my situation:

_____
_____
_____
_____

What actions will I take:

_____
_____
_____
_____

Notes

Date: _____ Pastor/Communicator: _____

Message Title: _____

_____
_____
_____
_____
_____
_____
_____
_____
_____
_____
_____
_____
_____
_____

What is God revealing:
_____
_____
_____
_____

How does this apply to my situation:
_____
_____
_____
_____

What actions will I take:
_____
_____
_____
_____

Notes

Date: _____ Pastor/Communicator: _____

Message Title: _____

_____

_____

_____

_____

_____

_____

_____

_____

_____

_____

_____

_____

What is God revealing:

_____

_____

_____

_____

How does this apply to my situation:

_____

_____

_____

_____

What actions will I take:

_____

_____

_____

_____

Notes

Date: _____   Pastor/Communicator: _____

Message Title: _____

_____

_____

_____

_____

_____

_____

_____

_____

_____

_____

_____

_____

_____

What is God revealing:

_____
_____
_____
_____
_____

How does this apply to my situation:

_____
_____
_____
_____
_____

What actions will I take:

_____
_____
_____
_____
_____

Notes

Date: _____ Pastor/Communicator: _____

Message Title: _____

_____

_____

_____

_____

_____

_____

_____

_____

_____

_____

_____

_____

_____

What is God revealing:

_____

_____

_____

_____

_____

How does this apply to my situation:

_____

_____

_____

_____

_____

What actions will I take:

_____

_____

_____

_____

_____

Notes

Date: _____   Pastor/Communicator: _____

Message Title: _____

_____
_____
_____
_____
_____
_____
_____
_____
_____
_____
_____
_____
_____
_____

What is God revealing:

_____
_____
_____
_____
_____

How does this apply to my situation:

_____
_____
_____
_____
_____

What actions will I take:

_____
_____
_____
_____
_____

Notes

Date: _____ Pastor/Communicator: _____

Message Title: _____

_____
_____
_____
_____
_____
_____
_____
_____
_____
_____
_____
_____
_____
_____
_____

What is God revealing:

_____

_____

_____

_____

How does this apply to my situation:

_____

_____

_____

_____

What actions will I take:

_____

_____

_____

_____

Copyright © 2020 Blkpawn Publishing

Published by Blkpawn Publishing
PO Box 161554
Ft Worth, TX 76161

For details on ordering information, contact the publisher at:
sales@blkpawnpublishing.com

All rights reserved. No part of this book may be reproduced or transmitted in any for by any means, electronic, or mechanical, including photocopy, recording or any information storage and retrieval system, without permission and writing from the publisher.

"Scripture quotations taken from the Amplified® Bible (AMP),
Copyright © 2015 by The Lockman Foundation
Used by permission. www.Lockman.org"

"Scripture quotations taken from the Free Bible Version (FBV),
This translation is directly from the Hebrew and Greek text. It is licensed under a Creative Commons Attribution-NoDerivs 4.0 Unported License."

Scripture quotations marked (NIV) are taken from the Holy Bible, New International Version®, NIV®. Copyright © 1973, 1978, 1984, 2011 by Biblica, Inc.™ Used by permission of Zondervan. All rights reserved worldwide. www.zondervan.com The "NIV" and "New International Version" are trademarks registered in the United States Patent and Trademark Office by Biblica, Inc.™

First paperback edition December 2020

Book design by Kiwitta Paschal
Cover Designed by macrovector / Freepik

ISBN 978-1-7362869-0-6 (paperback)

www.ingramcontent.com/pod-product-compliance
Lightning Source LLC
Chambersburg PA
CBHW072205100526
44589CB00015B/2373